# Pand Box

Written by Pauline Cartwright
Illustrated by Margaret Power

One fine sunny day, some bees that were looking for a new home found an old shed on the Martins' farm. They got in through spaces between the old boards, and they seemed to want to stay there. Mr. Martin thought about smoking them out, or trying to get them to join the bees he already had in a dozen hives on the farm. But he decided to leave them alone. They weren't causing any trouble.

He warned his son, Andy, to leave the shed door shut tight and not to bother the bees in any way. Andy sat and watched them buzzing in and out through the spaces in the walls. There were a lot of bees in there! He certainly wasn't thinking about opening that door. It would be like opening Pandora's box.*

Andy smiled at the thought and went to find his father's beekeeper's hat and some paint. He came back to the shed wearing the hat (just in case there were some unfriendly bees) and carrying an old bucket of red paint and a brush. Then he carefully painted the words "PANDORA'S BOX" in large letters on the door.

* Turn to page 30 to find out about the ancient Greek myth, *Pandora's Box*.

The bees didn't seem to notice Andy, but Mrs. Haines, who came and did housework for Andy and his father, stopped shaking the mat at the back door.

"What are you doing, Andy? I hope you're not writing bad words!" she said.

"Dad and I have been reading Greek myths. Do you know the one about Pandora?" Andy asked her.

But Mrs. Haines just shook her head and went back inside. She thought a television in the house would give the boy a more normal way to spend his time. But Mr. Martin had never bothered to buy a TV. Andy knew that made Mrs. Haines – and other people, too – think that his father was a little different.

Andy didn't really care what people thought. Sometimes he wished they had a television, but most of the time he was glad his father wasn't like other fathers. Andy was allowed to do many things that other parents never let their children do.

He didn't know of anyone else who was allowed to paint pictures all over their bedroom walls. Andy loved doing that. It gave him enough space to paint all the pictures that he had in his head.

He didn't know of other children who were allowed to read at the table during dinner. He thought that there probably wasn't anyone in his class who had read as many books as he had. And he didn't know anyone else who was allowed to stay up so late. If Andy didn't stay up late, he would never have the chance to go and look at the night sky with his father. He loved listening to his father explain the moon and the stars and the planets to him.

Maybe his father wasn't a very successful farmer, but he had planted a wonderful forest of trees in the valley, and they always seemed to have enough money. Maybe there wasn't enough for new cars or exciting vacations, but Andy always got to do the things he really wanted to do.

Today, Andy's father was working in a field at the back of the farm, and Andy knew he wouldn't be home until dinnertime. His father had left a note that said he was looking for a sick goat.

Andy looked to see what Mrs. Haines had made for dinner, and then he started to pour himself some juice. The walk home from school had made him hot and tired.

Suddenly, Andy had a strange feeling. He stopped pouring the juice. Someone else was in the room.

Andy turned slowly and then jumped when he saw a man in the doorway. The juice in Andy's glass splashed onto his bare legs.

"Is anyone else home?" asked the man.

"My dad's at the back of the...." Suddenly Andy thought that he shouldn't tell this man where his father was. He shouldn't let him know that there was no one else in the house. He noticed the man's dirty hair and the way his eyes looked quickly around the room. The man made him nervous.

"So, he's at the back of the farm?" The man smiled in a mean way. "And your mother's not here either, is she? I saw her drive off. You're all alone, aren't you, kid?"

The man was definitely a stranger because he didn't know that Andy's mother was dead. Andy decided not to tell the stranger that the woman he had seen was Mrs. Haines, their housekeeper.

How long had the man been watching the house? How long had he been standing in the doorway?

Andy was very nervous, but he tried to be brave. "You didn't knock," he told the man. "You shouldn't walk in without knocking!"

The man's expression changed to a frown. Suddenly, he moved toward Andy. His hand reached out and grabbed Andy by the shirt collar. He lifted Andy right off his feet.

"You don't talk to me like that, kid – understand?"

He put Andy back down. Andy stared at him without saying a word. He was trying not to show his fear, but his heart was pounding. He noticed the man's big black boots, his leather jacket, and his dirty jeans. The man's legs were very long.

If Andy could just reach the door and escape the man's long arms, he still wouldn't be able to escape those long legs. Suddenly, the man's arm shot out again and grabbed Andy's collar. He pushed Andy in front of him into the hallway and toward the bedroom.

"Don't try to fool around with me. Just tell me where the money is. I need some cash, kid."

In the bedroom, the man let Andy go and began pulling drawers open, throwing things on the floor, searching wildly for something.

Andy stood silently. This was such a strange experience. His brain seemed to be running in circles. He was filled with fear and shock and a powerful need to do something. He couldn't just stand and watch this man and do nothing.

15

Then Andy thought about what an amazing real-life drama this was. They didn't need a TV – nothing on television could compare with this! The thought brought a small smile to his face.

When the man saw the smile on Andy's face, he reached out and hit him on the shoulder. "You think it's funny, don't you, kid? Think it's funny that I haven't found anything yet? Just you wait – I'll find what's here."

Andy was furious. This man had walked into their house, uninvited! He was looking through all his father's things! And now the man had hit him!

Andy saw that in a moment, the man would reach the drawer where his father kept some things that had belonged to Andy's mother. There were some letters, a silver necklace, a string of pearls, and photographs. Andy hated the idea of this horrible man touching any of those lovely things.

The anger that filled Andy's head seemed to make a buzzing sound in his ears. Suddenly, through the buzzing, an idea burst into his mind.

"I know where he keeps it," Andy said to the man. "I know where the money is."

The man quickly turned to face him. "Now you're starting to think, kid." The man's eyes narrowed as he left the chest of drawers and walked toward Andy. "Where is it?"

Andy was good at inventing stories. He had spent his life reading stories, listening to stories, writing stories. Now a story had come into his mind, and he easily found the words for it.

"My father's not like other people. He doesn't put his money in the bank. He says he can't trust banks."

The man's eyes widened. "Is that true?"

"Oh, yes!" lied Andy. "My father's different. He doesn't keep his money in the house, either. He says that robbers always look in the house, so he doesn't hide it in here."

"Are you going to tell me he buries it in the yard?" the man asked suspiciously. He wasn't sure if he could trust Andy. His hands went out to grab Andy again, but he stopped, waiting to hear more.

"Oh, no. He doesn't bury it. He just puts it in a place where people wouldn't think of looking. But I know where it is. I'll show you, if you'll go away after you get it."

The man put an arm around Andy's shoulders. "Sure, sure,
I'll go as soon as I get the money. Now, where's this hiding place?"

Andy began walking out of the bedroom and felt better when
the man's arm dropped from his shoulders. "It's not far.
It's in an old shed. People don't think of looking for money
in an old shed. You didn't think of it, did you?" Andy kept talking
and talking as he walked down the hallway, through the kitchen,
and out the door.

"My father puts all his money into old socks, and then he puts the old socks inside bags of – of onions." Andy lied again. "Then he hangs up the bags of onions in the shed, and nobody knows the money is there."

"Your father sure is different, kid. You can tell by the look of this whole place." The man looked quickly around the yard and all over the house. "What's that painted on the door? Those words – what do they mean?"

Andy was pretty sure that the man didn't know the name "Pandora." So he lied again. "Ah, Pandora. Well, it's a kind of onion. It's the name of the onions Dad stores in the bags where he keeps the money."

23

When he reached the shed, Andy said, "I'll slide back the bolt, but you'll have to push the door open. It's really hard to open." Andy was sliding the bolt back.

"Stay right there, kid. You're coming in with me." The man's voice was full of distrust.

"Sure. I'll come in and show you the bags, if you promise to go afterwards. My mother will be home soon. She only went to the store."

Andy took a step back. "The door is really, really hard to open. It gets stuck. You'll have to push it as hard as you can."

Andy was happy to see that the man was stepping back, drawing up his shoulders, and turning himself sideways. He was getting ready to use all his force against the door.

The man threw himself against the door, and Andy ran up
the path as fast as he could. Andy could feel his heart beating.
As he ran, he heard lots of noise – the sound of the door (which
wasn't stuck at all) as it flew open, a great crash against the far
wall, a wild yell from the man, and the sounds of boxes inside
the shed falling down on top of him.

As Andy reached the back door of the house, he heard
an angry roar that became a kind of scream, and he turned
to watch the man coming out of the shed. At first the man was
down on his hands and knees, but then he got up and started
to run, trying to escape. There were hundreds of angry, buzzing
bees all around him.

Andy ran in through the open back door. He locked it behind him and then ran to a window. He opened it quickly as the man ran across the yard. "The river's down the hill!" he shouted. "It's across the field and down the hill! Jump in there!"

Then he slammed the window shut. He watched as the man ran crazily in circles around the yard and started across the field, yelling the whole time. The bees went with him, like a dark cloud around his head. Then Andy went to the telephone in the hall and called the police.

There was a picture in Andy's mind of a man with long, whirling arms and legs, with flying hair, with an open mouth yelling. He decided to paint it the next day on the shed door, right under the words, "PANDORA'S BOX."

# The Myth of Pandora's Box

**The following story is a myth from ancient Greece.**

Once upon a time, there was a child named Epimetheus (Epa-ME-thee-us). One day, another child arrived at his door. Her name was Pandora, and she was very curious.

The first thing Pandora saw when she got to Epimetheus' little house was a beautiful box. It was made of bronze, and it was big and shiny and golden.

"What's in the box?" asked Pandora.

Epimetheus answered, "I don't know. It's a secret. The box was left here by someone, and I don't know what's inside."

"Where did it come from? Who gave it to you?" Pandora asked eagerly.

Epimetheus shook his head and replied, "That's a secret, too."

Pandora begged Epimetheus to tell her more. But Epimetheus told her nothing else about the box.

"How can I tell you anything more, Pandora?" said Epimetheus. "I don't know any more about what's inside."

Pandora said, "Well, we could open it and see for ourselves!"

"We aren't *allowed* to open the box, Pandora," he answered.

Days went by, and Pandora and Epimetheus became good friends. They had no worries, and life was good. But Pandora could not stop thinking about the box.

"How did the box get here?" she asked Epimetheus.
So he finally told her that a messenger with wings on his feet had brought the box.

"Maybe he brought the box for us and maybe it's full of new clothes and toys and presents! Let's take a look," said Pandora.

Epimetheus said he didn't want to open the box. Then he went outside to play, and Pandora was left alone in the little house.

Pandora looked at the box. Then she walked around it. She looked at the latch that held the box closed. She knelt down in front of the box and tried to move the latch. It clicked open.

"I'll open up the cover just a tiny bit," she said. And she did.

When Pandora opened the box, a terrible thing happened. Dark clouds started to fly out of the box, carrying troubles that had never been in the world before. Horrible, scary things like sickness, war, and cruelty escaped from the box and flew around the little house.

"Help!" cried Pandora. She tried to push the cover of the box back down, but she could not keep the clouds of terrible troubles from escaping. Finally, she jumped up and, using all of her strength, managed to close the box.

Epimetheus heard Pandora calling for help. He ran back to see what was wrong. All the terrible troubles that Pandora had released were circling around the little house in a frightening dark cloud. He ran inside the house, and there was Pandora, sitting on top of the box and looking scared.

"What happened, Pandora?" Epimetheus asked.

"It was horrible!" she replied. "I lifted the cover just a tiny bit and all those terrible things escaped."

While Pandora and Epimetheus watched, the dark cloud flew away to spread trouble all over the world.

"This is terrible!" said Epimetheus.

Then Pandora felt something moving in the box. From inside, a sweet little voice called, "Please let me out!" Pandora jumped down and opened the box one more time.

Inside the box, there was only one thing left – hope. Hope remained when all the horrible troubles that had escaped from the box spread unhappiness throughout the world.

Today, you might hear someone use the expression, "A Pandora's box." They are talking about something that seems good at first, but could lead to an awful lot of trouble.

If the future doesn't look good, people sometimes try to be optimistic and say, "There's always hope." When you hear these expressions, remember the myth of Pandora's box!